ISBN 978-0-260-73247-7
PIBN 11114227

This book is a reproduction of an important historical work. Forgotten Books uses
state-of-the-art technology to digitally reconstruct the work, preserving the original format
whilst repairing imperfections present in the aged copy. In rare cases, an imperfection in
the original, such as a blemish or missing page, may be replicated in our edition. We do,
however, repair the vast majority of imperfections successfully; any imperfections that
remain are intentionally left to preserve the state of such historical works.

1 MONTH OF
FREE
READING

at
www.ForgottenBooks.com

By purchasing this book you are eligible for one month membership to ForgottenBooks.com, giving you unlimited access to our entire collection of over 1,000,000 titles via our web site and mobile apps.

To claim your free month visit:

www.forgottenbooks.com/free1114227

English
Français
Deutsche
Italiano
Español
Português

www.forgottenbooks.com

Mythology Photography **Fiction**
Fishing Christianity **Art** Cooking
Essays Buddhism Freemasonry
Medicine **Biology** Music **Ancient**
Egypt Evolution Carpentry Physics
Dance Geology **Mathematics** Fitness
Shakespeare **Folklore** Yoga Marketing
Confidence Immortality Biographies
Poetry **Psychology** Witchcraft
Electronics Chemistry History **Law**
Accounting **Philosophy** Anthropology
Alchemy Drama Quantum Mechanics
Atheism Sexual Health **Ancient History**
Entrepreneurship Languages Sport
Paleontology Needlework Islam
Metaphysics Investment Archaeology
Parenting Statistics Criminology
Motivational

United States
Department of
Agriculture

Forest
Service

North Central
Forest Experiment
Station

Resource Bulletin
NC-156

The Timber Resource
of the Chippewa
National Forest

Neal P. Kingsley and Robert E. Brittain

'90

North Central Forest Experiment Station
Forest Service—U.S. Department of Agriculture
1992 Folwell Avenue
St. Paul, Minnesota 55108
Manuscript approved for publication July 28, 1994
1994

CONTENTS

Page

The Timber Resource of the Chippewa National Forest

Neal P. Kingsley and Robert E. Brittain

Note: *Data from new forest inventories are often compared with data from earlier inventories to determine trends in forest resources. However, for the comparisons to be valid, the procedures used in the two inventories must be similar. As a result of our ongoing efforts to improve the efficiency and reliability of the inventory, several changes in procedures and definitions have occurred since 1980. Because some of these changes will make it inappropriate to directly compare the 1990 data with those published for 1980, data from the 1980 inventory have been reprocessed using the 1990 procedures. Please refer to the section labeled "Comparing Minnesota's Fifth Inventory with the Fourth Inventory" for more details.*

The Chippewa is the oldest of the Eastern Region's National Forests. In 1902, the Minnesota Federation of Women's Clubs secured passage of the Morris Act, protecting the area as a Forest Preserve. In 1908, President Theodore Roosevelt proclaimed this same area as the Minnesota National Forest. Later the name was changed to reflect the region's dominant Indian influence. Most of the Leech Lake Indian

Neal P. Kingsley, Research Forester, received his bachelor's degree in forestry in 1961 and his master's degree in forest economics in 1963 from the University of New Hampshire. He spent 25 years with the Northeastern Forest Experiment Station before joining the North Central Forest Experiment Station in 1988 as Program Manager of the Forest Inventory and Analysis project.

Robert E. Brittain received his bachelor's degree in forest management from West Virginia University in 1961. He began his Forest Service career on the Chequamegon National Forest in Wisconsin. He worked on the Mark Twain and Monongahela National Forests before joining the staff of the Chippewa as a Forest Silviculturist in 1977.

Reservation lies within the Forest's outer boundary. More than 5,000 cultural resource sites are believed to exist on the Chippewa. Managing these sites in cooperation with the Indian community is an integral part of managing this National Forest.

The Chippewa National Forest has been managed for more than 75 years under the multiple-use concept of forest management. This concept integrates all the Forest's resources—wildlife, water, recreation, cultural heritage, and timber. Wildlife, especially white tail deer, grouse, and many species of waterfowl abound. The Chippewa is home to one of the largest concentrations of bald eagles in the United States and to small populations of timber wolves and moose.

Water is everywhere on the Chippewa. More than 900 miles of rivers and streams and more than 162,000 acres of wetlands provide essential habitat for over 200 species of fish and wildlife including walleye pike, northern pike, eagles, ospreys, herons, loons, and many other wetland birds. The management and protection of this water resource are important functions of the Forest.

With an abundance of water, wildlife, and scenic beauty, the Chippewa is becoming an increasingly important recreational resource. The Forest provides campgrounds, picnic areas, boat launch sites, and trails for recreationists. In 1990, the Chippewa had an estimated 4.5 million recreation visitors.

In addition to providing wildlife habitat, watershed protection, recreational opportunities, and taking care of cultural treasures, the Chippewa has sold an average of 142,000 cords of wood annually over the past 10 years to Minnesota's forest-based industries. This report is about the Chippewa's role as a supplier of timber. Not all the volume and growth reported here is in fact available for timber harvesting. Because management of the Chippewa is guided by a comprehensive management plan, some areas are managed for non-timber benefits and others are not currently available for harvesting to allow them to develop into desired forest ecosystems.

Forest Area

The Chippewa National Forest encompasses 662.9 thousand acres of land in north-central Minnesota. Nearly 88 percent of this land—581.6 thousand acres—is classed as forest land. Of this, 567.2 thousand acres is classed as timberland, forest land that is capable of producing a sustained crop of wood and that is not withdrawn from timber harvesting. Under the Forest's management plan, 480 thousand acres are considered suitable for harvesting.

The aspen forest type dominates the Chippewa's landscape, covering 42 percent of the Forest's timberland—238.6 thousand acres (fig. 1). Despite the predominance of aspen, the Forest still contains an impressive mix of species. However, no other forest type accounts for more than 10 percent of the Forest's area. The second most abundant type, maple-basswood, covers only 55.4 thousand acres. The third and fourth ranked types, red pine and black spruce, cover 51.3 and 37.5 thousand acres, respectively[1].

Timber on the Chippewa is maturing (fig. 2). In 1990, 40 percent—226.6 thousand acres—of the Forest's timberland was in sawtimber-size stands, up from 30 percent in 1980. Likewise, the area of poletimber stands declined from 45 to 29 percent—162.7 thousand acres. While there was more timberland in sawtimber-size stands in 1990 than in 1980, there was also more in seedling-sapling stands. The area of seedling-sapling stands was 177.8 thousand acres—31 percent of the timberland—up from 24 percent in 1980. This indicates that older stands are being replaced with younger, faster growing stands. When aspen stands mature, they decline very quickly as mortality begins to exceed growth. If this process is allowed to continue, these stands will become dominated by other species and the type will change. In

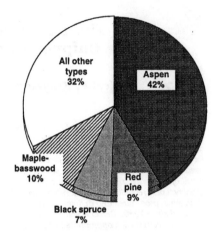

Figure 1.—*Area of timberland by major forest type, Chippewa National Forest, 1990.*

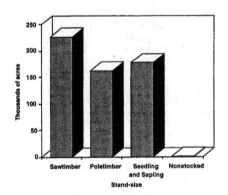

Figure 2.—*Area of timberland by stand-size class, Chippewa National Forest, 1990.*

---

[1]*Forest type in this inventory is determined in a different manner than in the Chippewa's stand examinations. For this reason, forest types may vary from those shown in the Forest's management plan.*

this region, this succession usually leads to maple-basswood or balsam fir stands, depending on the site. To maintain an abundance of aspen, an important timber and wildlife species, these older declining stands must be replaced with young stands of aspen before they change type. All in all, the distribution of stand-size classes in 1990 was better than in 1980.

Timber Volume

Timber volume on the Chippewa increased by 9 percent since 1980 to just over 743 million cubic feet in 1990 (fig. 3). The Forest's most abundant species, quaking aspen, gained only 2 percent to 193.7 million cubic feet. However, the Forest's second most abundant species, red pine, increased 86 percent to 120.5 million cubic feet. Another important softwood, white pine, gained 46 percent to 25.3 million cubic feet. Black spruce showed a gain of 174 percent. However, most of this black spruce undoubtedly resulted from the reclassification of many wet sites from unproductive to marginally productive forest land.

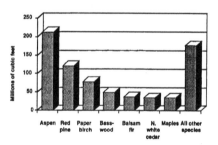

Figure 3.—*Volume of growing stock by major species, Chippewa National Forest, 1990.*

Overall, the total volume in hardwood species has remained essentially unchanged since 1980. The only major hardwood species to show a significant gain was basswood, which stood at 48.8 million cubic feet, up about 34 percent since the last inventory. Thus, it would appear that softwood species are becoming a more significant component of the Forest.

The volume of sawtimber on the Chippewa stood at 2.0 billion board feet, up 28 percent since 1980. The volume of aspen sawtimber, at 558 million board feet, was up 38 percent, reflecting maturity or overmaturity of many aspen stands. The volume of red and white pine sawtimber also showed significant increases. Red pine, at 521 million board feet, was up 58 percent. White pine, at 126.4 million board feet, was up 75 percent. Among the major hardwoods other than aspen, basswood showed the most significant gain with a rise of 77 percent to 119 million board feet.

Timber Growth and Removals

Net annual growth on the Chippewa is slightly higher than in the surrounding region of the State. During the period 1980-1990, net annual growth averaged 19.2 million cubic feet or 33.8 cubic feet per acre of timberland (fig. 4). During this same period, the surrounding region averaged 28.4 cubic feet per acre per year. Thus, while net annual growth in the region averaged 2.2 percent of the average inventory, it averaged 2.7 percent on the Forest. Growing sites on the Chippewa are not significantly better than in the region as a whole. Therefore, the higher growth on the National Forest probably reflects a higher level of forest management there. Net annual growth of sawtimber averaged 81.5 million board feet or about 4.5 percent of the sawtimber inventory.

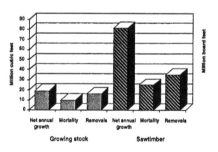

Figure 4.—*Volume of net annual growth, mortality, and removals, growing stock and sawtimber, Chippewa National Forest, 1990.*

Average annual removals of growing stock during the 1980-1990 period were just over 16 million cubic feet, about 2.3 percent of the average annual inventory and 85 percent of the net annual growth. Average annual removals of sawtimber present a somewhat different story that reflects the fiber versus saw-log economy of the region. Average annual removals of sawtimber from 1980 to 1990 were 35.3 million board feet, only 43 percent of the average net annual growth of sawtimber and slightly less than 2 percent of the sawtimber inventory. In a fiber-oriented forest economy, there is little premium for large trees.

During the 1980-1990 period, the mortality of growing stock averaged just under 10 million cubic feet, slightly more than half the average net annual growth. Mortality of sawtimber averaged 18 million board feet, less than half the average net annual growth of sawtimber.

Although the level of mortality of growing stock on the Chippewa is not excessively high, much

of it can be traced to the high level of mortality of aspen and, to a lesser degree, of paper birch. Mortality of aspen growing stock, at 3.9 million cubic feet, averaged 76 percent of net annual growth. This reflects the high number of mature and overmature stands referred to earlier. When aspen stands reach maturity, they decline rapidly; mortality of aspen often exceeds growth as other species dominate the stand. To maintain aspen stands, it is necessary to harvest before they reach this stage so they can be replaced by young fast growing stands. That this is being done on the Chippewa is evidenced by the fact that removals of aspen averaged more than 8 million cubic feet during the period between inventories, 3 million in excess of net annual growth. We can expect to see a significant increase in aspen growth in the future as these older stands are harvested and regenerated. The situation for paper birch is similar. In the absence of strong markets for birch, many stands have reached the 70- to 80-year age class and have begun to decline.

APPENDIX

ACCURACY OF THE SURVEY

Forest Inventory and Analysis information is based on a sampling procedure designed to provide reliable statistics at the State and Survey Unit levels. Consequently, the reported figures are estimates only. A measure of reliability of these figures is given by sampling errors. These sampling errors mean that the chances are two out of three that if a 100-percent inventory had been taken, using the same methods, the results would have been within the limits indicated.

For example, the estimated growing-stock volume in the Chippewa National Forest in 1990, 743.2 million cubic feet, has a sampling error of ±3.70 percent (±27.5 million cubic feet). The growing-stock volume from a 100-percent inventory would be expected to fall between 715.7 and 770.7 million cubic feet (743.2 ± 27.5) there being a one in three chance that this is not the case.

The following tabulation shows the sampling errors for the Chippewa National Forest inventory:

Item	Forest totals	Sampling error
Growing stock	(Million cubic feet)	(Percent)
Volume (1990)	743.2	3.70
Average annual growth (1980-1990)	19.2	5.50
Average annual removals (1980-1990)	16.3	21.20
Sawtimber	(Million board feet)	
Volume (1990)	2,031.9	5.00
Average annual growth (1980-1990)	81.5	5.80
Average annual removals (1980-1990)	35.3	25.40
Timberland area (1990)	(Thousand acres) 567.2	2.00

As survey data are broken down into sections smaller than Survey Unit totals, the sampling error increases. For example, the sampling error for timberland area in a particular county is higher than that for total timberland area on the Forest. This tabulation shows the sampling error for Forest totals. To use this information for data smaller than Forest totals, compute error estimates with the following formula:

$$Error = \frac{(SE) \sqrt{\text{National Forest total area or volume}}}{\sqrt{\text{Volume or area smaller than national Forest total}}}$$

E = sampling error in percent
SE = National Forest total error for area or volume

For example, to compute the error on the volume of quaking aspen in the Forest, proceed as follows:

The total volume of quaking aspen in the Forest from table 8 = 193.7 million cubic feet

The total volume of all growing stock in the Forest from table 8 = 743.2 million cubic feet

The total error for growing-stock volume from the above tabulation = 3.70 percent

Using the above formula:

$$Error = \frac{(3.70) \ \sqrt{743.2}}{\sqrt{193.7}}$$

$$= \pm 7.25 \text{ percent}$$

Survey Procedures

The 1990 Minnesota survey used a growth model-enhanced, two-phase sample design. This sampling scheme and associated estimators are similar to sampling with partial replacement (SPR), in that a set of randomly located plots is available for remeasurement and a random set of new plots is established and measured. A significant feature of the new Minnesota design is stratification for disturbance on the old sample and use of a growth model to improve regression estimates made on old undisturbed forest plots as shown in the following diagram (fig. 5). The growth model used in the Minnesota survey design was the Lake States Stand and Tree Evaluation and Modeling System (STEMS)[2].

---

[2] Belcher, David W.; Holdaway, Margaret R.; Brand, Gary J. 1982. A description of STEMS—the Stand and Tree Evaluation and Modeling System. Gen. Tech. Rep. NC-79. St. Paul, MN: U.S. Department of Agriculture, Forest Service, North Central Forest Experiment Station. 18 p.

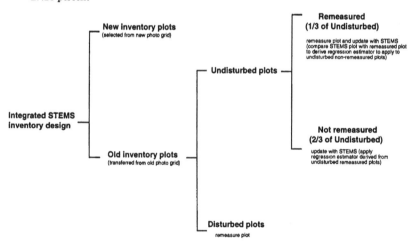

Figure 5.—*Overview of the Minnesota sample design.*

These were the major steps in the new survey design:

1. Aerial photography (Phase 1)

In this phase two sets of random points were located on current aerial photography. The first is a set of new photo plots, and the second is a set of relocated old ground plot locations from the 1977 inventory. Photos were 1:58,000 scale color infrared National High Altitude Photography Program (NHAP) prints purchased by the Minnesota Department of Natural Resources (MDNR) from the U.S. Geological Survey. In addition, MDNR provided 35mm true color prints at a scale of 1:15,840 of all of the 1977 ground plot locations. These 35mm prints were used in addition to the NHAP prints to aid in disturbance detection of the 1977 ground plot locations. The year of photography for each county in the Forest is shown below.

County	Date	
	NHAP	35mm
Beltrami	1981-1983	1987
Cass	1981	1988
Itasca	1981	1987-1988

The locations of the plots used in the 1980 inventory were transferred to these new photographs. The photographs were then assembled into township mosaics, and a systematic grid of 121 one-acre photo plots (each plot representing approximately 190.4 acres) was overlaid on each township mosaic. Each of these photo plots was examined by aerial photogrammetrists and classified stereoscopically, based on land use. If trees were present, forest type and stand size-density class were recorded. All the 1980 ground plot locations were also examined for disturbance (logging, fire, catastrophic mortality, etc.) with the aid of the 35mm photography. After this examination, all the old "disturbed" sample locations, a one-third sample of the old "undisturbed" sample locations, and a sample of the new photo plots were sent to the field for survey crews to verify the photo classification and to take further measurements. In all, 3,346 new photo plots and 169 ground plot locations from the 1980 inventory were examined for the National Forest and were classified as shown in the tabulation at the top of the next column:

Photo land class	Photo plots
Timberland	2,823
Reserved timberland	—
Other forest land	52
Questionable	50
Nonforest with trees	40
Nonforest without trees	364
Water	17
All classes	3,346

2. Plot measurements (Phase 2)

On plots classified as timberland, wooded pasture, or windbreak (at least 120 feet wide), a ground plot was established, remeasured, or modeled. Each old plot sent to the field for remeasurement that could not be relocated was replaced with a new plot at the approximate location of the old one. Each ground plot consists of a 10-point cluster covering approximately 1 acre. At each point, trees 5.0 inches or more in d.b.h. were sampled on a 37.5 Basal Area Factor (BAF) variable-radius plot, and trees less than 5.0 inches d.b.h. were sampled on a 1/300-acre fixed-radius plot. The measurement procedure for the new and old sample locations was as follows:

a. New inventory plots

A random sample of the new photo plots was selected for field measurement. Ground plots were established, and measures of current classification such as land use, forest type, and ownership as well as the size and condition of all trees on the plot were recorded. These locations were monumented for future remeasurement.

b. Old inventory plots

These plots were established, monumented, and measured as part of the 1980 field inventory. The procedures for these old plot locations were different from those for the new plots. Old plots were classed as "undisturbed" or "disturbed" in the aerial photo phase sampling process. All disturbed plots and one-third of the undisturbed plots were remeasured to obtain estimates of current condition and changes since the last inventory. All trees measured on these plots in 1980 were remeasured or otherwise accounted for, and all new trees were identified and measured.

All sample plots that were forested at the time of the 1980 inventory and determined to be undisturbed until this inventory were projected to the current time using the Stand and Tree Evaluation and Modeling System (STEMS). This procedure gives projected estimates of current volume and growth for these undisturbed plots. The comparison of the projected and observed values on the one-third sample of the undisturbed forest plots that were re-measured provided local calibration data to adjust the projected values of the undis-turbed plots that were not remeasured. The adjustment procedure is a modified version of the method described by Smith[3].

The old sample plots that were not forested in 1980 and that were determined to be undisturbed until the current inventory (no evidence of conversion to another land use) were also subsampled (field checked) at the one-third rate. Any changes in land use to forest detected on these plots were used to adjust the two-thirds sample of these plots not field checked. The field check of these points in the National Forest indicated that no adjustment was necessary.

The undisturbed plots that were not remeasured play a crucial role in the new survey design. These plots, after careful examination comparing past and current aerial photography, were determined to be undisturbed and had conditions that could be simulated by STEMS. The STEMS growth model was used to "grow" the old plot and tree data to produce an estimate of current data. Thus, these plots were treated as ground plots, even though they were never visited. The plot record for each modeled plot was sent to the field for verifi-cation of current ownership information.

All old plots classified as disturbed were sent to the field for remeasurement to assess and verify changes since the last inventory. Disturbance refers to any change on a plot that can be detected on aerial photos and that the STEMS growth processor cannot predict, such as catastrophic mortality, cutting, seedling stands, and land use change.

The estimation procedure for computing statis-tics from this sampling design was more compli-cated than the simple two-phase estimation procedure used in the past. In fact, this proce-dure yielded two independent samples, one coming from the new photo points and the other from the old photo points that were remeasured or modeled. The following tabulation summa-rizes the distribution of all ground plots for the new inventory design by type of plot:

Ground land use class	Old plots remeasured	Old plots updated	New plots	Total plots
Timberland	149	4	257	410
Reserved forest land	1	—	1	2
Other forest land	2	1	5	8
Nonforest with trees	3	—	2	5
Nonforest without trees	12	2	34	48
Water	2	—	3	5
Total	169	7	302	478

[3] Smith, W. Brad. 1983. Adjusting the STEMS regional growth models to improve local predictions. Res. Note NC-297. St. Paul, MN: U.S. Department of Agricul-ture, Forest Service, North Central Forest Experiment Station. 5 p.

3. Area estimates

The total area of National Forest land was supplied by the Forest staff. Subsequent area estimates were made using two-phase estimation methods. In this type of estimation, a preliminary estimate of area by land use is made from the aerial photographs (Phase 1) and corrected by the plot measurements (Phase 2). A complete description of this estimation method is presented by Loetsch and Haller (1964)[4].

Area estimates within the Chippewa National Forest were determined in the same way as other lands but were verified by comparison with National Forest compartment examination records maintained by the Forest Timber Management Staff. This is an intensive area inventory system in which, over a period of years, each stand in the Forest is mapped on aerial photographs and then classified by ground visits.

4. Volume estimates

Estimates of volume per acre were made from the trees measured or modeled on the 10-point plots. Estimates of volume per acre were multiplied by the area estimates to obtain estimates of total volume. Net cubic foot volumes are based on a modification of the method presented by Hahn[5] for use in the Lake States. For the Minnesota inventory, the merchantable height equation presented was used in conjunction with Stone's equation to estimate gross volume. This estimate was then corrected by species for variation in bark and cull volume to yield an estimate of net volume.

The Forest Service reports all board foot volume in International 1/4-inch rule. In Minnesota, the Scribner log rule is commonly used. Scribner log rule conversion factors were derived

from full tree measurements taken throughout the Lake States (Michigan, Wisconsin, and Minnesota) and an equation developed by Wiant and Castenaeda (1977)[6]. The factors (multipliers) used here to convert board foot International volumes to the Scribner rule are shown in the following tabulation:

D.B.H. (inches)	Scribner rule conversion factor	
	Softwoods	Hardwoods
9.0-10.9	0.7830	—
11.0-12.9	.8287	0.8317
13.0-14.9	.8577	.8611
15.0-16.9	.8784	.8827
17.0-18.9	.8945	.8999
19.0-20.9	.9079	.9132
21.0-22.9	.9168	.9239
23.0-24.9	.9240	.9325
25.0-26.9	.9299	.9396
27.0-28.9	.9321	.9454
29.0+	.9357	.9544

5. Growth and mortality estimates

On remeasured plots, estimates of growth and mortality per acre come from the remeasured diameters of trees and from observation of trees that died between inventories. Growth reported as the average net annual growth between the two inventories (1980 and 1990) is computed from data on remeasurement plots and modeled plots using methods presented by VanDeusen et al.[7] Mortality is also average net annual for the remeasurement period. On new plots, where trees were not remeasured, estimates of growth and mortality were obtained by using STEMS to project the growth and mortality of trees for 1 year. Growth and mortality estimates for old undisturbed plots that were updated were derived in the same manner as for remeasured plots. The STEMS growth model was adjusted by Survey Unit to meet local conditions, using data from the undisturbed remeasurement

[4] Loetsch, F.; Haller, K.E. 1964. Forest inventory, volume I, statistics of forest inventory and information from aerial photographs. BLV Verlagsgesellschaft Munch Basle Vienna. 436 p.

[5] Hahn, Jerold T. 1984. Tree volume and biomass equations for the Lake States. Res. Pap. NC-250. St. Paul, MN: U.S. Department of Agriculture, Forest Service, North Central Forest Experiment Station. 10 p.

[6] Wiant, Harry V., Jr.; Castenaeda, Froylan. 1977. Mesavage and Girard's volume tables formulated. BLM4. Denver, CO: U.S. Department of the Interior, Bureau of Land Management, Denver Service Center. 4 p.

[7] VanDeusen, P.C.; Dell, T.R.; Thomas, C.E. 1986. Volume growth estimation from permanent horizontal points. Forest Science. 32: 415-422.

plots. As with volume, total growth and mortality estimates were obtained by multiplying the per acre estimates by area estimates. Current annual growth for 1990 was computed by using the adjusted STEMS model to grow all current inventory plots for 1 year.

6. Average annual removals estimates

Average annual growing-stock and sawtimber removals (1980 to 1990) were estimated only from the remeasured plots; new plots were not used to estimate removals. These estimates are obtained from trees measured in the last survey and cut or otherwise removed from the timberland base. Because remeasurement plots make up about one-half of the total ground plots, average annual removals estimates have greater sampling errors than volume and growth estimates.

COMPARING MINNESOTA'S FIFTH INVENTORY WITH THE FOURTH INVENTORY

The following paragraphs highlight some of the procedural changes since the last inventory to assist the reader in analyzing data from this report:

A new volume estimation procedure has been developed for the Lake States (see Survey Procedures), and this procedure was used to compute the 1990 volumes and also to recompute the 1980 volume for growth calculations. Although the adjustment will differ by Survey Unit and species, the recomputed 1980 growing-stock and board foot volumes will generally be greater than those reported for 1980.

Mortality figures published in the 1980 inventory report were based on field estimates of the number of trees that died in the 3 years before the inventory. Information gathered on remeasurement plots during the current inventory was used to adjust the 1979 mortality figures. This adjustment will also affect the estimate of net growth for the 1980 inventory.

Past surveys used only growing-stock trees to determine stand-size class. Current survey procedures require that stand-size class be determined on the basis of all live trees. Therefore, direct comparisons of current inventory data to old inventory data by stand-size class may be misleading.

LOG GRADES

In Minnesota the butt log of every sawtimber sample tree was graded for quality on approximately one-third of the sample plots. The volume yield by log grade for species in this sample was used to distribute the volume of trees in the ungraded sample into log-grade classes by species group.

Logs were graded on the basis of external characteristics as indicators of quality. Hardwood species were graded according to "A guide to hardwood log grading" (1973)[8]. The best 12-foot section of the lowest 16-foot hardwood log, or the best 12-foot upper section if the butt log did not meet minimum log-grade standards, was graded as follows:

---

[8] Rast, Everette D.; Sonderman, David L.; Gammon, Glenn L. 1973. A guide to hardwood log grading. Gen. Tech. Rep. NE-1. Upper Darby, PA: U.S. Department of Agriculture, Forest Service, Northeastern Forest Experiment Station. 31 p.

Forest Service standard grades for hardwood factory saw logs

Grading Factors		Specifications							
		Log grade 1			Log grade 2		Log grade 3		
		Butts only	Butts & uppers		Butts & uppers				Butts & uppers
Position in tree									
Scaling diameter, inches		13-15[1]	16-19	20+	11+[2]	12+			
Length without trim, feet			10+		10+	8-9	10-11	12+	8+
Required clear cuttings[3] of each of three best faces[4]	Min. length, feet	7	5	3	3	3	3	3	2
	Max. number		2	2	2	2	2	3	No limit
	Min. proportion of log length required in clear cutting	5/6	5/6	5/6	2/3	3/4	2/3	2/3	1/2
Maximum sweep & crook allowance	For logs with less than one-fourth of end in sound defects	15 percent			30 percent				50 percent
	For logs with more than one-fourth of end in sound defects	10 percent			20 percent				35 percent
Maximum scaling deduction		40 percent[5]			50 percent[6]				50 percent

1 Ash and basswood butts can be 12 inches if they otherwise meet requirements for small #1's.
2 Ten-inch logs of all species can be #2 if they otherwise meet requirements for small #1's.
3 A clear cutting is a portion of a face, extending the width of the face, that is free of defects.
4 A face is one-fourth of the surface of the log as divided lengthwise.
5 Otherwise #1 logs with 41-60 percent deductions can be #2.
6 Otherwise #2 logs with 51-60 percent deductions can be #3.

Forest Service standard specifications for hardwood construction logs (tie and timber logs)[1]

Position in tree	Butts and uppers
Min. diameter, small end	8 inches +
Min. length without trim	8 feet
Clear cuttings	No requirements
Sweep allowance	One-fourth of the diameter at the small end for each 8 feet of length.
Sound surface defects:	
Single knots	Any number, if no one knot has an average diameter above the callus in excess of one-third of the log diameter at point of occurrence.
Whorled knots	Any number, if the sum of knot diameters above the callus does not exceed one-third of the log diameter at point of occurrence.
Holes	Any number, provided none has a diameter over one-third of the log diameter at point of occurrence and none extends more than 3 inches into included timber[2].
Unsound surface defects:	Same requirements as for sound defects if they extend into included timber. No limit if they do not.

[1] *These specifications are minimum for the class. If, from a group of logs, factory logs are selected first, thus leaving only nonfactory logs from which to select construction logs, then the quality range of the construction logs so selected is limited, and the class may be considered a grade. If selection for construction logs is given first priority, it may be necessary to subdivide the class into grades.*
[2] *Included timber is always square, and dimension is judged from small end.*

LOG GRADES FOR EASTERN WHITE PINE

Log grade	Minimum size[1] Diameter	Length	Sweep or crook allowance	Total cull allowance including sweep	Maximum weevil injury	Allowable knot size (inches)[2] on three best faces or minimum clearness on four faces
	(Inches)	(Feet)	(Percent)	(Percent)	(Number)	(Inches)
1	12 & 13	8-16	20	50	0	Four faces clear full length
	14+	10-16	20	50	0	Two faces clear full length, or four faces clear 50 percent length (6 feet min. length)[3]
2	6+	8-16	30	50	0	Sound knots l.e.[4] D.6 and less than 3 inches[5]
						Unsound knots: l.e. 1-1/2 inches and for: butt, log l.e. D/12 upper logs l.e. D/10, or four faces clear 50 percent of length
3	6+	8-16	40	50	8-foot logs 1 weevil	Sound knots l.e. D/3 and less than 5 inches
					10-foot+ logs: 2 weevils	Unsound knots l.e. D/6 and less than 2-1/2 inches
4	6+	8-16	50	50	No limit	No limit

[1] Plus trim.
[2] Disregard all knots less than 1/2-inch diameter in all grades.
[3] The sum of the diameter of sound knots plus twice the sum of the diameter of unsound knots (in inches) is less than or equal to half of the diameter of the log (inches.)
[4] l.e. means less than or equal to.
[5] D means d.i.b. of log at location of knot.

12

LOG GRADES FOR JACK PINE AND RED PINE

Grade 1: Logs with three or four clear faces.[1]

Grade 2: Logs with one or two clear faces.

Grade 3: Logs with no clear faces.

After the tentative log grade is established from above, the log will be degraded one grade for each of the following, except that no log can be degraded below grade 3. Net scale after deduction for defect must be at least 50 percent of the gross contents of the log.

1. *Sweep.* Degrade any tentative 1 or 2 log one grade if sweep amounts to 3 or more inches and equals or exceeds one-third of the diameter inside bark at small end.

2. *Heart rot.* Degrade any tentative 1 or 2 log one grade if conk, massed hyphae, or other evidence of advanced heart rot is found anywhere in it.

[1]*A face is one-fourth of the circumference in width extending full length of the log. Clear faces are those free of: knots measuring more than 1/2-inch in diameter, overgrown knots of any size, and holes more than 1/4-inch in diameter. Faces may be rotated to obtain the maximum number of clear ones.*

LOG GRADES FOR ALL OTHER SOFTWOOD LOGS

Grade 1

1. Logs must be 16 inches in diameter or larger, 10 feet in length or longer, and with deduction for defect not over 30 percent of gross scale.

2. Logs must be at least 75 percent clear on each of three faces.

3. All knots outside clear cutting must be sound and not more than 2-1/2 inches in size.

Grade 2

1. Logs must be 12 inches in diameter or larger, 10 feet in length or longer, and with a net scale after deduction for defect of at least 50 percent of the gross scale deducted for defect.

2. Logs must be at least 50 percent clear on each of three faces or 75 percent clear on two faces.

Grade 3

1. Logs must be 6 inches in diameter or larger, 8 feet in length or longer, and with a net scale after deduction for defect of at least 50 percent of the gross contents of the log.

Note: A) *Diameters are diameter inside bark (d.i.b.) at small end of log.*
B) *Percent clear refers to percent clear in one continuous section.*

METRIC EQUIVALENTS OF UNITS USED IN THIS REPORT

1 acre = 4,046.86 square meters or 0.405 hectare.
1,000 acres = 405 hectares.
1 cubic foot = 0.0283 cubic meter.
1 foot = 30.48 centimeters or 0.3048 meter.
1 inch = 25.4 millimeters, 2.54 centimeters, or 0.0254 meter.
1 pound = 0.454 kilograms.
1 ton = 0.907 metric tons.

TREE SPECIES GROUPS ON THE CHIPPEWA NATIONAL FOREST[9]

SOFTWOODS

Eastern white pine .... *Pinus strobus*
Red pine ....: *Pinus resinosa*
Jack pine .... *Pinus banksiana*
White spruce .... *Picea glauca*
Black spruce .... *Picea mariana*
Balsam fir .... *Abies balsamea*
Tamarack .... *Larix laricina*
Northern white-cedar .... *Thuja occidentalis*
Other softwoods:
Eastern redcedar ....*Juniperus virginiana*
Scotch pine .... *Pinus sylvestris*

HARDWOODS

White oak[10]
White oak .... *Quercus alba*
Bur oak .... *Quercus macrocarpa*
Red oak[10]
Northern red oak .... *Quercus rubra*
Northern pin oak .... *Quercus ellipsoidalis*
Black oak .... *Quercus velutina*
Hickory[10]
Shagbark hickory .... *Carya ovata*
Bitternut hickory .... *Carya cordiformis*
Hard maple[10]
Black maple .... *Acer nigrum*
Sugar maple .... *Acer saccharum*
Soft maple[11]
Red maple .... *Acer rubrum*
Silver maple .... *Acer saccharinum*

---

[9] *The common and scientific names are based on: Little, Elbert L. 1979. Checklist of native and naturalized trees of the United States. Agric. Handb. 541. Washington, DC: U.S. Department of Agriculture, Forest Service. 385 p.*

[10] *This species or species group is considered a hard hardwood, with an average specific gravity greater than or equal to 0.50.*

[11] *This species or species group is considered a soft hardwood, with an average specific gravity of less than 0.50.*

14

Birch
Paper birch[11] .... *Betula papyrifera*
Yellow birch[10] .... *Betula alleghaniensis*
Ash[10]
Black ash .... *Fraxinus nigra*
Green ash .... *Fraxinus pennsylvanica*
Balsam poplar[11] .... *Populus balsamifera*
Aspen[11]
Bigtooth aspen .... *Populus grandidentata*
Quaking aspen .... *Populus tremuloides*
Cottonwood[11] .... *Populus deltoides*
Basswood[11] .... *Tilia americana*
Black walnut[10] .... *Juglans nigra*
Black cherry[11] .... *Prunus serotina*
Butternut[11] ....*Juglans cinerea*
Elm
American elm[11] .... *Ulmus americana*
Slippery elm[11] .... *Ulmus rubra*
Rock elm[10] .... *Ulmus thomasii*
Hackberry[11] .... *Celtis occidentalis*
Black willow[11] .... *Salix nigra*
Other hardwoods
Boxelder[11] .... *Acer negundo*
Black locust[10] .... *Robinia pseudoacacia*
Red mulberry[11] .... *Morus rubra*
Honeylocust[10] .... *Gleditsia triacanthos*
Northern catalpa[10] .... *Catalpa speciosa*
Noncommercial species
Eastern hophornbeam .... *Ostrya virginiana*
Apple .... *Malus* spp.
American hornbeam .... *Carpinus caroliniana*
Wild plum .... *Prunus* spp.
Hawthorn .... *Crataegus* spp.

DEFINITION OF TERMS

Average annual removals from growing stock.—The average net growing-stock volume in growing-stock trees removed annually for forest products (including roundwood products and logging residues) and for other uses (see Other removals). Average annual removals of growing stock are reported for a period of several years (1980 to 1990 in this report) and are based on information obtained from remeasurement plots (see Survey Procedures in Appendix).

Average annual removals from sawtimber.—The average net board foot sawtimber volume of live sawtimber trees removed annually for forest products (including roundwood products and other uses (see Other removals)). Average annual removals of sawtimber are reported for a period of several years (1980 to 1990 in this report) and are based on information obtained from remeasurement plots (see Survey Procedures in Appendix).

Commercial species.—Tree species presently or prospectively suitable for industrial wood products. (Note: Excludes species of typically small size, poor form, or inferior quality such as hophornbeam, mountain maple, and chokecherry).

Commercial forest land.—(See Timberland).

Cord.—One standard cord is 128 cubic feet of stacked wood, including bark and air space. Cubic feet can be converted to standard cords by dividing by 79.

Cull.—Portions of a tree that are unusable for industrial wood products because of rot, missing or dead material, or other defect.

Diameter class.—A classification of trees based on diameter outside bark, measured at breast height (d.b.h.). Two-inch diameter classes are commonly used in Forest Inventory and Analysis, with the even inch the approximate midpoint for a class. For example, the 6-inch class includes trees 5.0 through 6.9 inches d.b.h.

Diameter at breast height (d.b.h.).—The outside bark diameter at 4.5 feet (1.37m) above the forest floor on the uphill side of the tree. For determining breast height, the forest floor includes the duff layer that may be present, but does not include unincorporated woody debris that may rise above the ground line.

Forest land.—Land at least 16.7 percent stocked by forest trees of any size, or formerly having had such tree cover, and not currently developed for nonforest use. (Note: Stocking is measured by comparing specified standards with basal area and/or number of trees, age or size, and spacing.) The minimum area for classification of forest land is 1 acre. Roadside, streamside, and shelterbelt strips of timber must have a crown width of at least 120 feet to qualify as forest land. Unimproved roads and trails, streams, or other bodies of water or clearings in forest areas shall be classed as forest if less than 120 feet wide. (See Tree, Land, Timberland, Reserved forest land, Other forest land, and Stocking.)

Forest type.—A classification of forest land based on the species forming a plurality of live tree stocking. Major forest types in the State are:

Jack pine.—Forests in which jack pine comprises a plurality of the stocking. (Common associates include eastern white pine, red pine, aspen, birch, and maple.)

Red pine.—Forests in which red pine comprises a plurality of the stocking. (Common associates include eastern white pine, jack pine, aspen, birch, and maple.)

White pine.—Forests in which eastern white pine comprises a plurality of the stocking. (Common associates include red pine, jack pine, aspen, birch, and maple.)

Balsam fir.—Forests in which balsam fir and white spruce comprise a plurality of the stocking with balsam fir the most common. (Common associates include aspen, maple, birch, northern white-cedar, and tamarack.)

White spruce.—Forests in which white spruce and balsam fir comprise a plurality of the stocking with white spruce the most common. (Common associates include aspen, maple, birch, northern white-cedar, and tamarack.)

Black spruce.—Forests in which swamp conifers comprise a plurality of the stocking with black spruce the most common. (Common associates include tamarack and northern white-cedar.)

Northern white-cedar.—Forests in which swamp conifers comprise a plurality of the stocking with northern white-cedar the most common. (Common associates include tamarack and black spruce.)

Tamarack.—Forests in which swamp conifers comprise a plurality of the stocking with tamarack the most common. (Common associates include black spruce and northern white-cedar.)

Oak-hickory.—Forests in which oaks or hickories, singly or in combination, comprise a plurality of the stocking. (Common associates include jack pine, elm, and maple.)

Elm-ash-soft maple.—Forests in which lowland elm, ash, red maple, silver maple, and cottonwood, singly or in combination, comprise a plurality of the stocking. (Common associates include birches, spruce, and balsam fir.)

Maple-basswood.—Forests in which sugar maple, basswood, yellow birch, upland American elm, and red maple, singly or in combination, comprise a plurality of the stocking. (Common associates include white pine, elm, and basswood.)

Aspen.—Forests in which quaking aspen or bigtooth aspen, singly or in combination, comprise a plurality of the stocking. (Common associates include balsam poplar, balsam fir, and paper birch.)

Paper birch.—Forests in which paper birch comprises a plurality of the stocking. (Common associates include maple, aspen, and balsam fir.)

Balsam poplar.—Forests in which balsam poplar comprised a plurality of the stocking. (Common associates include aspen, elm, and ash.)

Growing-stock tree.—A live tree of commercial species that meets specified standards of size, quality, and merchantability. (Note: Excludes rough, rotten, and dead trees.)

Growing-stock volume.—Net volume in cubic feet of growing-stock trees 5.0 inches d.b.h. and over, from 1 foot above the ground to a minimum 4.0 inch top diameter outside bark of the central stem or to the point where the central stem breaks into limbs.

Hard hardwoods.—Hardwood species with an average specific gravity greater than 0.50 such as oaks, hard maple, hickories, and ash.

Hardwoods.—Dicotyledonous trees, usually broad-leaved and deciduous. (See Soft hardwoods and Hard hardwoods.)

Land.—*A. Bureau of the Census.* Dry land and land temporarily or partly covered by water such as marshes, swamps, and river flood plains (omitting tidal flats below mean high tide); streams, sloughs, estuaries, and canals less than one-eighth of a statute mile wide; and lakes, reservoirs, and ponds less than 40 acres in area.

B. Forest Inventory and Analysis. The same as the Bureau of the Census, except minimum width of streams, etc., is 120 feet and minimum size of lakes, etc., is 1 acre.

Log grade.—A log classification based on external characteristics as indicators of quality or value. (See Appendix for specific grading factors used.)

Marsh.—Nonforest land that characteristically supports low, generally herbaceous or shrubby vegetation and that is intermittently covered with water.

Merchantable.—Refers to a pulpwood or saw-log section that meets pulpwood or saw-log specifications, respectively.

Mortality.—The volume of sound wood in growing-stock and sawtimber trees that die annually.

National Forest land.—Federal land that has been legally designated as National Forest or purchase units, and other land administered by the USDA Forest Service.

Net annual growth of growing stock.—The annual change in volume of sound wood in live sawtimber and poletimber trees and the total volume of trees entering these classes through ingrowth, less volume losses resulting from natural causes.

Net annual growth of sawtimber.—The annual change in the volume of live sawtimber trees and the total volume of trees reaching sawtimber size, less volume losses resulting from natural causes.

Net volume.—Gross volume less deductions for rot, sweep, or other defect affecting use for timber products.

Noncommercial species.—Tree species of typically small size, poor form, or inferior quality that normally do not develop into trees suitable for industrial wood products.

Nonforest land.—Land that has never supported forests, and land formerly forested where use for timber management is precluded by development for other uses. (Note: Includes areas used for crops, improved pasture, residential areas, city parks, improved roads of any width and adjoining clearings, powerline clearings of any width, and 1- to 40-acre areas of water classified by the Bureau of the Census as land. If intermingled in forest areas, unimproved roads and nonforest strips must be more than 120 feet wide and more than 1 acre in area to qualify as nonforest land.)

a. Nonforest land without trees.—Nonforest land with no live trees present.

b. Nonforest land with trees.—Nonforest land with one or more trees per acre at least 5 inches d.b.h.

Nonstocked land.—Forest land less than 16.7 percent stocked with all live trees.

Other forest land.—Forest land not capable of producing 20 cubic feet per acre per year of industrial wood crops under natural conditions and not associated with urban or rural development. These sites often contain tree species that are not currently utilized for industrial wood production or trees of poor form, small size, or inferior quality that are unfit for industrial products. Unproductivity may be the result of adverse site conditions such as sterile soil, dry climate, poor drainage, high elevation, and rockiness. This land is not withdrawn from timber utilization.

Other removals.—Growing-stock trees removed but not utilized for products, or trees left standing but "removed" from the timberland classification by land use change. Examples are removals from cultural operations such as timber stand improvement work, land clearing, and changes in land use.

Poletimber stand.—(See Stand-size class.)

Poletimber tree.—A growing-stock tree of commercial species at least 5.0 inches d.b.h. but smaller than sawtimber size.

Reserved forest land.—Forest land withdrawn from timber utilization through statute, administrative regulation, designation, or exclusive use for Christmas tree production, as indicated by annual shearing.

Rotten tree.—A tree that does not meet regional merchantability standards because of excessive unsound cull. May include noncommercial tree species.

Rough tree.—A tree that does not meet regional merchantability standards because of excessive sound cull. May include noncommercial tree species.

Salvable dead tree.—A standing or down dead tree considered merchantable by regional standards.

Sapling.—A live tree 1.0 to 5.0 inches d.b.h.

Sapling-seedling stand.—(See Stand-size class.)

Saw log.—A log meeting minimum standards of diameter, length, and defect, including logs at least 8 feet long, sound and straight and with a minimum diameter outside bark (d.o.b.) for softwoods of 7.0 inches (9.0 inches for hardwoods) or other combinations of size and defect specified by regional standards.

Saw-log portion.—That part of the bole of sawtimber trees between the stump and the saw-log top.

Saw-log top.—The point on the bole of sawtimber trees above which a saw log cannot be produced. The minimum saw-log top is 7.0 inches d.o.b. for softwoods and 9.0 inches d.o.b. for hardwoods.

Sawtimber stand.—(See Stand-size class.)

Sawtimber tree.—A growing-stock tree of commercial species containing at least a 12-foot saw log or two noncontiguous saw logs 8 feet or longer, and meeting regional specifications for freedom from defect. Softwoods must be at least 9.0 inches d.b.h. Hardwoods must be at least 11.0 inches d.b.h.

Sawtimber volume.—Net volume of the saw-log portion of live sawtimber in board feet, International 1/4-inch rule (unless specified otherwise) from stump to a minimum 7 inches top diameter outside bark (d.o.b.) for softwoods and a minimum 9 inches top d.o.b. for hardwoods.

Seedling.—A live tree less than 1.0 inch d.b.h. that is expected to survive. Only softwood seedlings more than 6 inches tall and hardwood seedlings more than 1 foot tall are counted.

Short-log (rough tree).—Sawtimber-size trees of commercial species that contain at least one merchantable 8- to 11-foot saw log but not a 12-foot saw log.

Site class.—A classification of forest lands in terms of inherent capacity to grow crops of industrial wood. The class identifies the potential growth in merchantable cubic feet/acre/year at culmination of mean annual increment of fully stocked natural stands.

Site index.—An expression of forest site quality based on the height of a free-growing dominant or codominant tree of a representative species in the forest type at age 50.

Soft hardwoods.—Hardwood species with an average specific gravity less than 0.50 such as gum, yellow-poplar, cottonwood, red maple, basswood, and willow.

Softwoods.—Coniferous trees, usually evergreen, having needles or scale-like leaves.

Stand.—A group of trees on a minimum of 1 acre of forest land that is stocked by forest trees of any size.

Stand-size class.—A classification of stocked (see Stocking) forest land based on the size class of live trees on the area; that is, sawtimber, poletimber, or saplings and seedlings.

   a. Sawtimber stands.—Stands with half or more of live stocking in sawtimber or poletimber trees, and with sawtimber stocking at least equal to poletimber stocking.

   b. Poletimber stands.—Stands with half or more live stocking in poletimber and/or sawtimber trees, and with poletimber stocking exceeding that of sawtimber.

   c. Sapling-seedling stands.—Stands with more than half of the live stocking in saplings and/or seedlings.

Stocking.—The degree of occupancy of land by live trees, measured by basal area and/or the number of trees in a stand by size or age and spacing, compared to the basal area and/or number of trees required to fully utilize the growth potential of the land; that is, the stocking standard.

   A stocking percent of 100 indicates full utilization of the site and is equivalent to 80 square feet of basal area per acre in trees 5.0 inches d.b.h. and larger. In a stand of trees less than 5 inches d.b.h., a stocking percent of 100 would indicate that the present number of trees is sufficient to produce 80 square feet of basal area per acre when the trees reach 5 inches d.b.h.

   Stands are grouped into the following stocking classes:

   Overstocked stands.—Stands in which stocking of live trees is 133 percent or more.

   Fully stocked stands.—Stands in which stocking of live trees is from 100.0 to 132.9 percent.

   Medium stocked stands.—Stands in which stocking of live trees is from 60.0 to 99.9 percent.

   Poorly stocked stands.—Stands in which stocking of live trees is from 16.7 to 59.9 percent.

   Nonstocked areas.—Timberland on which stocking of live trees is less than 16.7 percent.

Timberland.—Forest land that is producing or capable of producing in excess of 20 cubic feet per acre per year of industrial wood crops under natural conditions, that is not withdrawn from timber utilization, and that is not associated with urban or rural development. Currently inaccessible and inoperable areas are included (formerly commercial forest land).

Tree.—A woody plant usually having one or more perennial stems, a more or less definitely formed crown of foliage, and a height of at least 12 feet at maturity.

Tree size class.—A classification of trees based on diameter at breast height, including sawtimber trees, poletimber trees, saplings, and seedlings.

Upper stem portion.—That part of the bole of sawtimber trees above the saw-log top to a minimum top diameter of 4.0 inches outside bark or to the point where the central stem breaks into limbs.

Wooded strip.—An acre or more of natural continuous forest land that would otherwise meet survey standards for timberland except that it is less than 120 feet wide.

TABLE TITLES

Table 1.—Area of land by county and major land-use class, Chippewa National Forest, 1990

Table 2.—Area of land by district and major land-use class, Chippewa National Forest, 1990

Table 3.—Area of timberland by forest type and stand-size class, Chippewa National Forest, 1990

Table 4.—Area of timberland by forest type and potential productivity class, Chippewa National Forest, 1990

19

Table 1.--Area of land by county and major land-use class, Chippewa National Forest, 1990

(In thousand acres)

County	Land area	All forest land	Timber-land	Timberland as a percent of land area	Other forest land	Reserved forest land
				Forest land		
Beltrami	63.7	59.2	57.8	90.7	--	1.4
Cass	289.7	249.1	241.1	83.2	6.4	1.6
Itasca	309.5	273.3	268.3	86.7	5.0	--
All counties	662.9	581.6	567.2	85.6	11.4	3.0

Table 2.--Area of land by district and major land-use class, Chippewa National Forest, 1990

(In thousand acres)

National Forest District	Land area	All forest land	Timber-land	Timberland as a percent of land area	Other forest land	Reserved forest land
				Forest land		
Blackduck	127.8	119.5	116.8	91.4	2.7	--
Cass Lake	121.0	109.3	103.5	85.5	2.8	3.0
Deer River	173.1	154.8	148.9	86.0	5.9	--
Marcell	138.9	117.4	117.4	84.5	--	--
Walker	102.1	80.6	80.6	78.9	--	--
All districts	662.9	581.6	567.2	85.6	11.4	3.0

Table 3.--Area of timberland by forest type and stand-size class,
Chippewa National Forest, 1990

(In thousand acres)

| Forest type | All stands | Stand-size class | | | |
		Sawtimber	Poletimber	Seedling & sapling	Nonstocked
Jack pine	11.7	6.9	2.0	2.8	--
Red pine	51.3	28.9	13.0	9.4	--
White pine	4.0	4.0	--	--	
Balsam fir	23.6	9.1	6.7	7.8	--
White spruce	4.9	--	--	4.9	--
Black spruce	37.5	1.2	13.4	22.9	--
Northern white-cedar	26.0	12.3	12.8	0.9	--
Tamarack	22.6	8.1	8.5	6.0	--
Oak-hickory	7.2	2.7	3.3	1.2	--
Elm-ash-soft maple	33.8	9.6	9.9	14.3	--
Maple-basswood	55.4	38.2	12.5	4.7	--
Aspen	238.6	87.2	63.2	88.2	--
Paper birch	34.8	9.9	16.3	8.6	--
Balsam poplar	15.8	8.5	1.1	6.2	--
All types	567.2	226.6	162.7	177.9	--

Table 4.--Area of timberland by forest type and potential productivity class,
Chippewa National Forest, 1990

(In thousand acres)

Forest type	All classes	Potential productivity class (cu. ft. of growth per acre per year)				
		165+	120-164	85-119	50-84	20-49
Jack pine	11.7	--	--	0.9	8.0	2.8
Red pine	51.3	--	14.2	24.6	12.5	--
White pine	4.0	--	--	2.9	1.1	--
Balsam fir	23.6	--	--	--	1.1	22.5
White spruce	4.9	--	--	1.4	--	3.5
Black spruce	37.5	--	--	--	--	37.5
Northern white-cedar	26.0	--	--	--	--	26.0
Tamarack	22.6	--	--	--	--	22.6
Oak-hickory	7.2	--	--	--	6.2	1.0
Elm-ash-soft maple	3.8	--	--	--	2.3	31.5
Maple-basswood	5.4	--	--	13.2	14.0	28.2
Aspen	2 8.6	1.5	4.6	133.2	86.3	13.0
Paper birch	4.8	--	--	--	--	34.8
Balsam poplar	5.8	--	--	--	--	15.8
All types	567.2	1.5	18.8	176.2	131.5	239.2

Table 5.--Area of timberland by forest type and stocking class of growing-stock trees[1],
Chippewa National Forest, 1990

(In thousand acres)

Forest type	All classes	Stocking percent of growing-stock trees				
		Non-stocked	Poorly stocked	Moderately stocked	Fully stocked	Over-stocked
Jack pine	11.7	--	--	2.5	4.5	4.7
Red pine	51.3		--	9.0	11.8	30.5
White pine	4.0		--	1.3	1.1	1.6
Balsam fir	23.6	--	2.5	7.4	12.5	1.2
White spruce	4.9	--	3.5	--	1.4	--
Black spruce	37.5	1.2	--	5.2	17.1	14.
Northern white-cedar	26.0	--	1.5	8.9	11.1	4.0
Tamarack	22.6	--	7.1	9.6	3.9	2.9
Oak-hickory	7.2	1.2	--	2.3	3.7	--
Elm-ash-soft maple	3.8	--	6.2	15.5	10.7	1.4
Maple-basswood	5.4	--	2.3	20.7	26.2	6.2
Aspen	2 8.6	--	12.4	51.2	106.0	69.0
Paper birch	4.8	--	8.4	12.7	9.5	4.2
Balsam poplar	5.8	--	--	11.1	4.7	--
All types	567.2	2.4	43.9	157.4	224.2	139.3

[1] This table is based on the stocking percent of growing-stock trees rather than that of all live trees. To use the definitions of stocking for this table, replace the term "all live" by "growing-stock."

Table   Number of all live trees on timberland by species group and diameter class, Chippewa National Forest, 1990

(In thousand trees)

Species group	All classes	Diameter class (inches at breast height)											
		1.0-2.9	3.0-4.9	5.0-6.9	7.0-8.9	9.0-10.9	11.0-12.9	13.0-14.9	15.0-16.9	17.0-18.9	19.0-20.9	21.0-28.9	29.0+
Softwoods													
Jack pine	3,898	534	477	663	1,176	635	231	132	50	--	--	--	--
Red pine	15,605	2,628	2,694	3,308	2,613	1,752	1,041	633	426	207	151	152	8
White pine	1,936	324	519	193	222	143	199	128	42	49	19	90	--
White spruce	2,243	762	663	364	201	97	90	34	21	6	4	1	--
Black spruce	20,943	8,049	7,065	4,392	1,110	269	56	--	--	--	--	--	--
Balsam fir	44,741	27,747	9,150	4,760	1,975	731	265	100	13	--	--	2	--
Tamarack	9,647	3,078	2,520	2,111	1,338	386	173	30	7	--	4	--	--
Northern white-cedar	14,889	3,780	3,588	3,135	2,158	1,297	542	238	92	31	17	11	--
Total	113,902	46,902	26,676	18,926	10,793	5,310	2,597	1,295	651	293	195	256	8
Hardwoods													
Select white oak	6,047	2,670	1,314	922	658	273	114	67	17	8	4	--	--
Select red oak	4,146	1,797	522	140	811	277	174	59	47	11	3	5	--
Other red oak	116	63	--	--	--	10	6	6	4	4	--	--	--
Basswood	12,541	5,686	1,918	1,365	1,421	1,005	569	271	175	89	26	16	1
Yellow birch	917	450	219	126	42	25	14	18	8	7	6	2	--
Hard maple	16,208	10,144	3,075	1,072	841	318	288	163	165	70	57	15	--
Soft maple	13,016	6,504	2,922	2,048	1,012	353	131	24	16	6	6	--	--
Elm	4,144	2,815	792	271	129	64	33	19	19	2	--	--	--
Black ash	26,605	16,611	5,838	2,362	1,036	367	258	85	31	10	5	--	--
White and green ash	4,689	3,123	840	444	162	54	28	26	9	--	--	2	--
Balsam poplar	9,293	5,952	984	601	592	194	309	256	56	34	11	3	--
Bigtooth aspen	6,830	4,575	681	505	363	224	205	155	84	35	11	4	--
Quaking aspen	108,915	77,967	12,930	5,019	3,544	3,472	2,843	1,853	800	290	147	49	1
Paper birch	23,060	7,359	4,701	4,090	3,562	2,175	743	340	72	7	3	8	--
Black cherry	879	768	111	--	--	--	--	--	--	--	--	--	--
Other hardwoods	165	165	--	--	--	--	--	--	--	--	--	--	--
Noncommercial sp.	19,376	18,279	1,040	35	17	5	--	--	--	--	--	--	--
Total	256,947	164,928	37,887	19,300	14,190	9,116	5,738	3,342	1,503	573	265	104	1
All species	370,849	211,830	64,563	38,226	24,983	14,426	8,335	4,637	2,154	866	460	360	9

23

Table 7.--Number of growing-stock trees on timberland by species group and diameter class, Ottawa National Forest, 1990

(In thousand trees)

Species group	All classes	Diameter class (inches at breast height)											
		1.0-2.9	3.0-4.9	5.0-6.9	7.0-8.9	9.0-10.9	11.0-12.9	13.0-14.9	15.0-16.9	17.0-18.9	19.0-20.9	21.0-28.9	29.0+
Softwoods													
Jack pine	3,862	534	477	639	1,176	628	231	132	45	--	--	--	--
Red pine	15,541	2,628	2,694	3,265	2,602	1,752	1,031	633	426	207	151	152	--
White pine	1,915	324	519	193	222	134	192	128	42	49	17	88	7
White spruce	2,236	762	663	364	201	97	90	27	21	6	4	1	--
Black spruce	20,846	8,049	7,026	4,363	1,091	259	56	--	--	--	--	--	--
Balsam fir	44,068	27,297	9,024	4,740	1,942	718	258	100	9	--	--	2	--
Tamarack	9,352	3,078	2,520	1,951	1,293	334	135	30	7	--	4	--	--
Northern white-cedar	12,726	3,780	3,180	2,534	1,579	1,008	382	161	60	22	13	7	--
Total	110,566	46,452	26,103	18,049	10,106	4,930	2,375	1,211	610	284	189	250	7
Hardwoods													
Select white oak	5,760	2,628	1,251	814	598	263	114	67	13	8	4	5	--
Select red oak	3,999	1,749	522	440	776	257	148	54	34	11	3	--	--
Other red oak	96	63	--	--	--	10	15	--	4	4	--	--	--
Basswood	11,924	5,556	1,828	1,182	1,374	946	503	251	160	85	26	13	--
Yellow birch	839	450	219	96	24	8	7	14	8	7	6	4	--
Hard maple	14,523	9,884	2,526	814	645	205	183	98	90	44	30	--	--
Soft maple	11,860	6,504	2,712	1,722	581	223	93	12	13	--	--	2	--
Elm	4,094	2,788	792	271	118	56	33	15	19	2	--	3	--
Black ash	25,861	16,611	5,424	2,164	974	325	232	73	26	8	2	2	--
White and green ash	4,662	3,123	813	444	162	54	28	26	9	--	--	--	--
Balsam poplar	9,152	5,952	948	576	580	470	281	250	48	34	11	15	--
Bigtooth aspen	6,687	4,575	681	434	363	208	189	125	79	30	3	8	--
Quaking aspen	106,851	77,967	12,627	4,670	3,248	3,241	2,543	1,611	625	214	90	--	--
Paper birch	21,403	7,359	3,906	3,729	3,323	2,047	661	302	58	7	3	--	--
Black cherry	879	768	111	--	--	--	--	--	--	--	--	--	--
Other	165	165	--	--	--	--	--	--	--	--	--	--	--
Total	228,735	146,142	34,360	17,356	12,766	8,313	5,030	2,898	1,186	454	178	52	--
All species	339,301	192,594	60,463	35,405	22,872	13,243	7,405	4,109	1,796	738	367	302	7

Table 8.--Net volume of growing stock trees on timberland by species group and diameter class, Chippewa National Forest, 1990

(In thousand cubic feet)

Species group	All classes	Diameter class (inches at breast height)									
		5.0-6.9	7.0-8.9	9.0-10.9	11.0-12.9	13.0-14.9	15.0-16.9	17.0-18.9	19.0-20.9	21.0-28.9	29.0+
Softwoods											
Jack pine	22,607	1,698	6,270	6,202	3,658	3,244	1,535	---	---	---	---
Red pine	120,515	8,745	14,942	18,219	17,145	15,756	15,032	9,012	8,797	12,867	---
White pine	25,339	463	1,179	1,378	3,095	361	1,517	2,348	1,028	9,761	1,429
White spruce	7,043	1,098	1,256	1,085	1,554	697	654	334	256	109	---
Black spruce	21,395	11,318	6,209	2,809	902	---	---	---	---	157	---
Balsam fir	37,033	11,026	11,488	7,525	4,251	2,418	325	---	---	---	---
Tamarack	21,097	5,768	8,491	3,533	2,201	675	206	---	223	---	---
Northern white-cedar	34,841	5,563	8,117	9,003	5,177	3,591	1,666	684	634	406	---
Total	289,870	45,679	57,952	49,754	37,983	29,522	20,935	12,378	10,938	23,300	1,429
Hardwoods											
Select white oak	11,649	2,129	3,141	2,444	1,590	1,458	428	287	172	---	---
Select red oak	13,091	950	4,038	2,528	2,298	1,149	1,088	446	166	428	---
Other red oak	572	---	---	104	223	---	121	124	---	---	---
Basswood	48,758	3,507	8,592	10,521	8,648	6,160	5,322	3,581	1,256	1,171	---
Yellow birch	1,668	210	136	88	125	349	258	247	255	---	---
Hard maple	22,018	2,301	3,817	2,430	3,364	2,394	3,217	2,186	2,015	294	---
Soft maple	12,726	4,666	3,495	2,311	1,583	250	421	---	---	---	---
Elm	3,281	571	588	560	574	348	549	91	---	---	---
Black ash	21,886	5,573	5,982	3,450	3,704	1,190	831	326	106	124	---
White and green ash	4,022	1,027	895	620	428	614	263	---	---	175	---
Balsam poplar	23,768	1,554	3,218	4,856	4,621	5,708	1,491	1,486	564	270	---
Bigtooth aspen	18,031	1,296	2,414	2,559	3,589	3,483	2,978	1,545	167	---	---
Quaking aspen	193,677	12,236	20,448	36,937	45,438	40,902	21,495	9,828	5,287	1,106	---
Paper birch	78,180	11,683	21,489	22,831	11,541	7,590	1,987	317	166	576	---
Total	453,327	47,703	78,253	92,239	87,726	72,195	40,449	20,464	10,154	4,144	---
All species	743,197	93,382	136,205	141,993	125,709	101,717	61,384	32,842	21,092	27,444	1,429

25

Table 9.--Net volume of sawtimber trees on timberland by species group and diameter class, [?]ña National F rest, 1990

(In thousand board f eet)[1]

Species group	All classes	Diameter class (inches at breast height)							
		9.0-10.9	11.0-12.9	13.0-14.9	15.0-16.9	17.0-18.9	19.0-20.9	21.0-28.9	29.0+
Softwoods									
Jack pine	71,754	29,126	17,873	16,582	8,173	--	--	--	--
Red pine	521,201	91,625	87,961	83,262	81,917	50,345	50,251	75,840	--
Wte pine	126,515	6,274	14,529	15,379	7,776	12,446	5,578	55,980	8,553
Wte spruce	25,040	5,504	8,082	3,770	3,626	1,925	1,483	650	--
Black spruce	20,457	14,674	4,824	--	--	--	--	959	--
Balsam fir	70,821	35,759	20,930	12,403	1,729	--	--	--	--
Tamarack	35,264	17,761	11,462	3,607	1,145	--	1,289	--	--
Northern [w]- cedar	108,265	44,995	26,167	18,629	8,881	3,728	3,538	2,327	--
Total	979,317	245,718	191,828	153,632	113,247	68,444	62,139	135,756	8,553
Hardwoods									
Select [w]te oak	16,802	--	6,327	6,337	1,954	1,355	829	--	--
Select red oak	24,096	--	9,152	4,963	4,945	2,093	786	2,157	--
[?]er red oak	2,081	--	930	--	565	586	--	--	--
Basswood	118,999	--	36,407	27,813	25,099	17,428	6,225	6,027	--
Yellow [?]h	5,948	--	534	1,619	1,253	1,233	1,309	--	--
Hard maple	61,419	--	13,909	10,557	14,996	10,504	9,973	1,480	--
Soft [?]le	9,458	--	6,404	1,109	1,945	--	--	--	--
Elm	6,568	--	2,263	1,450	2,439	416	--	--	--
Black ash	31,240	--	16,055	8,365	4,029	1,615	542	634	--
White and green ash	6,584	--	1,765	2,722	1,221	--	--	876	--
Balsam poplar	63,679	--	19,552	25,774	7,006	7,146	2,806	1,395	--
[?]th aspen	53,806	--	15,439	15,847	14,129	7,540	851	--	--
[?]g aspen	557,808	--	191,889	185,051	101,191	47,740	26,312	5,625	--
Paper [?]th	94,112	--	46,694	33,226	9,081	1,491	796	2,824	--
Total	1,052,600	--	367,320	324,833	189,853	99,147	50,429	21,018	--
All species	2,031,917	245,718	559,148	478,465	303,100	167,591	112,568	156,774	8,553

[1] Int [?]tl 1/4-inch [?]e.

26

Table 10.--Net volume of growing stock and sawtimber on timberland by county and species group, Chippewa National Forest, 1990

| County | All species | Species group | | | |
		Pine	Other softwoods	Soft hardwoods	Hard hardwoods
	- - - - - - - - - - - Thousand cubic feet of growing stock - - - - - - - - - - -				
Beltrami	50,092	2,637	14,606	27,312	5,537
Cass	343,971	77,915	43,199	182,370	40,487
Itasca	349,134	87,909	63,604	168,739	28,882
All counties	743,197	168,461	121,409	378,421	74,906
	- - - - - - - - - - - Thousand board feet [1] of sawtimber - - - - - - - - - - -				
Beltrami	104,020	8,084	24,108	64,239	7,589
Cass	914,811	327,510	92,423	422,573	72,305
Itasca	1,013,086	383,876	143,316	417,618	68,276
All counties	2,031,917	719,470	259,847	904,430	148,170

[1] International 1/4-inch rule.

Table 11.--Net volume of timber on timberland by class of timber and species group, Chippewa National Forest, 1990

(In thousand cubic feet)

Class of timber	All species	Species group			
		Pine	Other softwoods	Soft hardwoods	Hard hardwoods
Live trees					
Growing-stock trees					
Sawtimber					
Saw-log portion	335,002	121,759	44,002	145,618	23,623
Upper stem portion	86,369	13,405	7,073	56,471	9,420
Total	421,371	135,164	51,075	202,089	33,043
Poletimber	321,826	33,297	70,334	176,332	41,863
All growing-stock trees	743,197	168,461	121,409	378,421	74,906
Cull trees					
Short-log trees	11,204	195	962	6,186	3,861
Rough trees					
Sawtimber	10,226	128	1,749	5,029	3,320
Poletimber	15,642	169	2,473	9,167	3,833
Total	25,868	297	4,222	14,196	7,153
Rotten trees					
Sawtimber	14,072	230	2,761	9,188	1,893
Poletimber	4,372	--	1,100	2,560	712
Total	18,444	230	3,861	11,748	2,605
All cull trees	55,516	722	9,045	32,130	13,619
All live trees	798,713	169,183	130,454	410,551	88,525
Salvable dead trees					
Sawtimber	3,412	210	592	2,428	182
Poletimber	5,750	361	1,663	3,175	551
Total	9,162	571	2,255	5,603	733
All classes of timber	807,875	169,754	132,709	416,154	89,258

Table 12.--Net volume of sawtimber trees on timberland by species group and butt log grade,
Chippewa National Forest, 1990

(In thousand board feet)[1]

| Species group | All grades | Butt log grade | | | Tie and timber |
		1	2	3	
Softwoods					
Jack pine	71,754	--	13,779	57,975	--
Red pine	521,201	111,270	104,170	305,761	
White pine	126,515	29,496	38,162	58,857	
White spruce	25,040	2,611	2,277	20,152	..
Black spruce	20,457	--	--	20,457	--
Balsam fir	70,821	--	1,130	69,691	--
Tamarack	35,264	--	3,630	31,634	--
Northern white-cedar	108,265	1,048	10,197	97,021	--
Total	979,317	144,424	173,345	661,548	--
Hardwoods					
Select white oak	16,802	3,047	1,363	10,831	1,562
Select red oak	24,096	--	--	24,096	--
Other red oak	2,081	--	--	2,081	--
Basswood	118,999	28,740	46,468	39,073	4,717
Yellow birch	5,948	--	--	--	5,948
Hard maple	61,419	19,100	34,803	5,418	2,099
Soft maple	9,458	--	1,759	6,438	1,261
Elm	6,568	--	4,430	2,138	--
Black ash	31,240	1,553	6,841	20,139	2,707
White and green ash	6,584	--	4,603	--	1,981
Balsam poplar	63,679	--	11,698	46,396	5,585
Bigtooth aspen	53,806	3,609	--	50,197	--
Quaking aspen	557,808	21,841	89,158	414,431	32,378
Paper birch	94,112	9,481	23,143	59,815	1,673
Total	1,052,600	87,370	224,265	681,053	59,912
All species	2,031,917	231,794	397,610	1,342,601	59,912

[1] International 1/4-inch rule.

Table 13.--Average net annual net growth, mortality, and removals of growing stock and sawtimber on national Forest, 1980-1990 net... by species group

Species group	Growing stock (Thousand cubic feet)			Sawtimber (Thousand board feet[2])		
	Net growth[1]	Mortality	Removals	Net growth[1]	Mortality	Removals
Softwoods						
Jack pine	182	477	97	1,80	1,318	83
Red pine	4,28	64	29	19,65	88	90
White pine	83	64	69	4,85	80	24
White spruce	86	33	311	2,59	64	1,723
Black spruce	218	145	94	72	83	--
Balsam fir	834	1,417	2,489	3,89	3,174	6,976
Tamarack	30	23	--	3,87	54	--
Northern white-cedar	63	54	148	3,66	93	644
All	7,624	2,777	3,447	38,713	6,734	10,490
Hardwoods						
Select white oak	89	39	27	640	56	79
Select red oak	91	25	247	1,90	311	199
Other red oak	8	5	--	30	17	--
Other oak	1,85	26	540	4,262	64	24
Yellow birch	15	34	28	15	84	--
Hard maple	544	96	87	1,62	92	56
Soft maple	66	29	83	64	74	--
Elm	-35	50	80	-342	994	1,30
Black ash	66	76	--	1,815	94	--
White and green ash	89	9	--	86	11	--
Balsam poplar	89	65	57	1,182	2,096	81
Bigtooth aspen	69	64	79	2,701	61	54
Quaking aspen	5,23	3,83	8,31	24,374	11,412	19,88
Paper birch	1,98	1,03	1,85	4,528	1,35	1,581
Total	11,567	7,184	12,894	42,817	18,091	24,782
All species	19,191	9,961	16,341	81,530	24,825	35,272

[1] An estimate of average gross growth may be computed by adding average mortality to average net growth.

[2] International 1/4-inch rule.

Kingsley, Neal P.; Brittain, Robert E.
   1994. **The timber resource of the Chippewa National Forest**. Resour.
   Bull. NC-156. St. Paul, MN: U.S. Department of Agriculture, Forest
   Service, North Central Forest Experiment Station. 30 p.
      Presents highlights and statistics on area, volume, growth, removals,
   and mortality from the 1990 forest inventory of the Chippewa National
   Forest.
   _____

   KEY WORDS: Area, volume, growth, removals, mortality.

Our job at the North Central Forest Experiment Station is discovering and creating new knowledge and technology in the field of natural resources and conveying this information to the people who can use it. As a new generation of forests emerges in our region, managers are confronted with two unique challenges: (1) Dealing with the great diversity in composition, quality, and ownership of the forests, and (2) Reconciling the conflicting demands of the people who use them. Helping the forest manager meet these challenges while protecting the environment is what research at North Central is all about.

NORTH CENTRAL
FOREST
EXPERIMENT STATION

CPSIA information can be obtained
at www.ICGtesting.com
Printed in the USA
BVHW090552211118
533509BV00027BA/2643/P